Jeremiah

*Daring to Hope
in an Unstable World*

A Bible Study by
Melissa Spoelstra

A Preview Book

Abingdon Press
Nashville

JEREMIAH:
DARING TO HOPE IN AN UNSTABLE WORLD
A BIBLE STUDY BY MELISSA SPOELSTRA –
A PREVIEW BOOK

Copyright © 2014 Abingdon Press

All rights reserved.

This book is printed on elemental chlorine-free paper.

ISBN 978-1-4267-8896-3

14 15 16 17 18 19 20 21 22 23 — 10 9 8 7 6 5 4 3 2 1

MANUFACTURED IN THE UNITED STATES OF AMERICA

Contents

Introduction 5

1. Raising the White Flag
Surrender 7

2. Recognizing Counterfeits and the Real Deal
Idolatry 17

3. Opening Our Ears
Listening 27

4. Staying Spiritually Sensitive
Heart Issues 36

5. Quitting the Blame Game
Personal Responsibility 45

6. Finding the Source of Our Hope
The Promised Messiah 54

Notes 64

Introduction

Life can be rough sometimes. Relationship struggles, health challenges, financial strain, and everyday demands can make life seem overwhelming. In those times, we're often tempted to respond with worry, fear, doubt, or bitterness. But God offers us a better choice. He calls us to surrender our wills to His and place all of our hope in Him.

This was the message of the prophet Jeremiah to the people of Judah—a message that is relevant to us, too. In this little book we will briefly explore six themes from Jeremiah's book that call us to put our hope in God alone. His writings encourage us that, because of our merciful and trustworthy God, hope-filled living is possible even in an unstable world.

Whether you're facing everyday challenges or a major crisis, you'll be encouraged by this snapshot preview of Jeremiah's message (which I explore in depth in my Bible study by the same title,

Jeremiah: Daring to Hope in an Unstable World). This man of God found himself in the midst of some very tough personal circumstances, yet he was able to keep his heart soft and hopeful through it all, trusting in the faithfulness of his God.

Join me as we discover God's promise of hope for our life and circumstances. Let's dare to hope together!

1

Raising the White Flag

Surrender

Have you ever felt like you are right on the brink? Just one more emotional strain, relational conflict, financial setback, or physical ailment will send you right over the edge, causing you to want to give in and quit. The prophet Jeremiah gives us a glimpse into the instability in his own life. He encountered family and ministry problems and even got into some legal trouble. It's easier to relate to a guy who certainly never pretended to have it altogether.

In the midst of Jeremiah's personal troubles and those of the surrounding culture, God gave him a message of surrender. But this call to surrender wasn't permission to just cop out and throw in the towel because of life's many hardships. Though it can be tempting to consider giving up as a parent, employee, or friend when the going gets tough, God calls us to a different kind of surrender. Through the prophet Jeremiah, God called the people of Judah to trust in Him by surrendering to His leading instead of trying to sort out life from their limited vantage point. And God gave Jeremiah plenty of opportunity to demonstrate how to do this. Again and again we see him looking to God's ways—made known through God's Word—over his own. Jeremiah said,

> *When I discovered your words, I devoured them.*
> *They are my joy and my heart's delight,*
> *for I bear your name,*
> *O LORD God of Heaven's Armies.*
>
> Jeremiah 15:16

We can learn a lot from this humble prophet's example. See if God's mega-theme of surrender through Jeremiah's life and writings echoes into your own white flag anxieties.

No Excuses

Jeremiah first responded to God's call with many reasons why he couldn't do what God asked of him. Choosing to obey God would cost him family relationships and social standing. He also told God he was too young.

> *"O Sovereign LORD," I said, "I can't speak for you! I'm too young!"*
> *The LORD replied, "Don't say, 'I'm too young,' for you must go wherever I send you and say whatever I tell you."*
>
> Jeremiah 1:6-7

Jeremiah made excuses, but God met every one with an assurance of His divine help and power. Eventually Jeremiah chose to believe and obey God in spite of his doubts and fears. In faith he followed God instead of giving in to his insecurities.

What nudging from God's Spirit have you been hearing lately? What plan has He revealed that will entail giving up some things you'd rather not? What excuses have you been making to get out of following God's clear leading? Jeremiah found that, although following God wasn't always easy, surrendering to God brought blessing while making excuses resulted in suffering consequences. As you consider what is holding you back from complete surrender to God, listen for God's voice of help and power assuring that He will empower you in every situation.

Surrender and Popularity

I know we like to pretend popularity was something we outgrew after high school, but many of us are still trying to find the right lunch table decades later. People-pleasing can influence our words, actions, and attitudes. We want people to like us. What about those times when totally yielding to God might upset our spouse, friends, or family members? God calls us to be faithful and obedient even when we must stand alone.

When Jeremiah boldly proclaimed God's message of surrender, he faced opposition from government leaders. In an effort to silence him, King Zedekiah ordered that he be placed in a large cistern. Jeremiah discovered that obedience doesn't always mean that life will be easy. He found himself at the bottom of a pit, realizing that God values character and obedience over personal comfort or human applause.

So the officials took Jeremiah from his cell and lowered him by ropes into an empty cistern in the prison yard. It belonged to Malkijah, a member of the royal family. There was no water in the cistern, but there was a thick layer of mud at the bottom, and Jeremiah sank down into it.

Jeremiah 38:6

How about you? How could completely yielding to the Lord in your life possibly affect those around you? Would they talk about you behind your back or think you've become a fanatic? What audience most greatly influences your daily decisions? Even though surrender won't always bring you popularity, God says He will bless you. His good plans might not always feel good in the moment, but obedience affords great long-term benefits. God promised to take care of Jeremiah and longs to shower us with His comfort as well.

Confirmation

Once we lay aside excuses and determine to please God above people, what if we still don't know what God is saying to us? Did we really hear God say we should quit our job, have another baby, or start a new ministry? Jeremiah's messages from God seemed so clear, yet even he sought confirmation. He stayed in close fellowship with God through honest dialogue coupled with deep study of His Word. While God can speak through anything or anyone, Jeremiah found God's confirmation most often through prayer, Scripture, and people. God also confirmed his word through Jeremiah by taking away his peace until he obeyed.

On one occasion, Jeremiah described the unrest he felt until he obeyed God with these words:

> *But if I say I'll never mention the L*ORD
> *   or speak in his name,*
> *his word burns in my heart like a fire.*
> *   It's like a fire in my bones!*
> *I am worn out trying to hold it in!*
> *   I can't do it!*

Jeremiah 20:9

I also have had times when I have asked God to direct me by giving me peace about a decision. When we weren't sure about a medical decision after praying, seeking counsel, and searching God's Word, I asked God to take away the overwhelming peace I felt about the procedure if it wasn't His leading. I felt His peace and lightness about proceeding when usually I would be fearful about this type of procedure, and I never regretted the choice later.

By following Jeremiah's example of intimate dialogue with God and careful study of God's Word, we can begin to discern whether a thought or idea is from the Holy Spirit or just our own desire. We also can find affirmation through people, circumstances, and when God "burns" His word in our hearts as He did in Jeremiah.

Defining Success

I find this thinking creeping into my own soul at times:

*I follow God = everything should go well
for me.*

But this is not biblical. The list is long of those who followed God and found hardship and difficulty. People mocked Noah for his boat project. Joseph's brothers put him in a pit and sold him. David hid in caves on the run for his life from King Saul. Jeremiah preached boldly but no one listened. His family rejected him, and his government imprisoned him.

We tend to define ourselves by our accomplishments, appearance, or intelligence. Yet Jeremiah shows us that even the most faithful followers can feel anxiety and depression and struggle to believe God through rough circumstances.

*I hurt with the hurt of my people.
I mourn and am overcome with grief.*
Jeremiah 8:21

Jeremiah didn't walk around pretending everything was great when it wasn't. He told God he was frustrated and confused. He asked God questions about justice, and then he listened to God's truth and comfort. He continued to trust as he worked through his complaints and doubts.

God invites us to come to Him and wrestle through our personal battles. These struggles don't mean we are unsuccessful Christians. Instead, they give us an opportunity to take our thoughts and emotions to God.

How do you define success in your life? Do you need compliant kids, a brilliant career, or a thriving ministry to feel a sense of worth and identity? According to Jeremiah's message, we find that true success is found in surrendering to God. God protected Jeremiah through their intimate relationship and taught him that eternal things matter more than temporary ones. Jeremiah realized that blessing comes from making the Lord your hope and confidence. By making the Lord your hope and confidence, you, too, can find the blessed life that leads to true success.

White Flag Anxiety

Jeremiah didn't try to sugarcoat his pain. He boldly told God that he wished he were never born. He called God's help uncertain and blamed Him for the suffering he endured. He held nothing back, and God responded to Jeremiah with comforting words, promising to take care of him.

Even though our circumstances may range from puzzling to downright depressing, we can know that God is the One who will take care of us, too. He doesn't leave us as orphans in a sea of questions, trials, and difficulties. He promises to walk with us.

In the midst of the anxiety that often results from surrendering control, God called Jeremiah to be an influencer. To do this, Jeremiah talked with God, devoured God's Word, and chose to stand alone—confident of the Lord's presence and power. God told Jeremiah,

> *"They will fight you, but they will fail.*
> > *For I am with you, and I will take care of you.*
> > *I, the LORD, have spoken!"*
>
> Jeremiah 1:19

Do you ever stuff your pain instead of honestly working through it with God? Have you joined in with the crowd regarding media choices, gossip, spending habits, or some other area of life when taking a stand could be unpopular? Where are you being dragged down instead of being a spokeswoman with God's message?

While raising the white flag isn't usually easy, its benefits are innumerable. Jesus surrendered to His Father's will and it resulted in our salvation. He calls us to take up our cross and follow Him. When we yield our plans to His, He can use us to bring His message of hope to an unstable world so desperately in need of it.

Where is God calling you to surrender today? Is there something you've been holding back because of fear or uncertainty—a relationship, a material item, a habit? Lay it down right now and hear God's tender words saying, "I will take care of you."

2.

Recognizing Counterfeits and the Real Deal

Idolatry

Have you ever struggled with riding the roller coaster of circumstances? When people seem to like us, stress levels are low, and things are going well in our world, we soar. But then we spiral downward when people are critical, money gets tight, or unexpected situations throw us off the ride completely. While God created us to experience emotions throughout life's ups and downs, we must be careful about what we have given ultimate place or priority in our lives. If we aren't careful, we might find ourselves living in despair because we put our hope in things that don't ultimately satisfy.

Jeremiah wrote about the danger of putting anything above God in our lives.

Idols are worthless; they are ridiculous lies!
> *On the day of reckoning they will all be*
> *destroyed.*
But the God of Israel is no idol!
> *He is the Creator of everything that exists,*
including Israel, his own special possession.
> *The L*ORD *of Heaven's Armies is his name!*

Jeremiah 10:15-16

Let's consider some of the ways that Jeremiah's prophecy helps us discern the difference between spiritual counterfeits and the real deal.

Forgetfulness

Jeremiah uses jewelry and wedding dresses as illustrations of things we rarely forget. He writes,

> *"Does a young woman forget her jewelry?*
> > *Does a bride hide her wedding dress?*
> *Yet for years on end*
> > *my people have forgotten me."*

Jeremiah 2:32

Even now I can remember the details of my dress, complete with lace and a long, satin train. I will never forget the large shoulder pads that were so in vogue back then. We remember things we value as important. Yet somehow in the craziness of our daily routines, schedules, meetings, and all the things we "must" do, God sometimes falls to the bottom of the list. We say He is first in our lives, but the focus of our time and attention might reveal that we sometimes settle for convenient counterfeits over true connection with our God.

Through Jeremiah's words of prophecy, God asks us to remember Him and not allow anything or anyone to take His place in our lives. What do you never forget because you value it so greatly? In what ways do you struggle with forgetting God? As we elevate God in our lives and value Him above all else, we will find ourselves less prone to forget. We'll remember His love, His justice, and His desire to have a deep relationship with us.

Spotting a Fake

God uses a word picture through Jeremiah to illustrate the difference between idols and Himself. Jeremiah says that God is like a fountain of living water—fresh, pure, and unlimited in supply. Then he likens idols to cracked cisterns. Cisterns were holes dug into the ground or rock for storing rainwater. And cisterns with cracks were completely useless for holding even dirty, stagnant water.

I find myself sometimes drawn to building cisterns. It keeps me busy, makes me feel like I'm contributing, and gives me the assurance of a backup plan just in case God doesn't come through. Yet these cisterns are always cracked—flawed. Without divine direction and supernatural guidance, we can spin our wheels in efforts that won't yield results. We need God's help to know where to invest our time, what opportunities to pursue, and how to make the best decisions.

When we go it alone—without drinking from the fountain of living water—we find that building cracked cisterns leaves us exhausted, dirty, and empty. Speaking through Jeremiah, God told how He felt about His people's cracked cisterns:

> *"For my people have done two evil things:*
> *They have abandoned me—*
> *the fountain of living water.*
> *And they have dug for themselves cracked cisterns*
> *that can hold no water at all!"*

Jeremiah 2:13

Trusting in God, obeying His Word, and walking closely with Him is what will quench our spiritual thirst. God offers us living water, but He never forces us to drink.

We need to evaluate which practices in our lives lead to drinking from the fountain of God and which lead us toward self-reliance and personal idolatry. While the rest of his culture built leaky cisterns, Jeremiah persevered in drinking from the fountain of God. As you lay aside your counterfeits and drink deeply from God's fountain, you'll find a quenching of your spiritual thirst that you'll want to share with others.

Counterfeit Consequences

God is a good daddy. He loves His children too much to leave us settling for empty substitutes. In Jeremiah's day, God gave clear instructions through His Word and issued warnings through His prophet when the people got off track spiritually. He was willing to stop His plans for exile if His people would stop their idolatrous ways.

"This is what the Lord of Heaven's Armies, the God of Israel, says: 'Even now, if you quit your evil ways, I will let you stay in your own land. . . . But I will be merciful only if you stop your evil thoughts and deeds and start treating each other with justice; only if you stop exploiting foreigners, orphans, and widows; only if you stop your murdering; and only if you stop harming yourselves by worshiping idols. Then I will let you stay in this land that I gave to your ancestors to keep forever.'"

Jeremiah 7: 3, 5-7

Eventually, after their continual disobedience, He followed through with the consequences He had warned them about—just as a loving parent would.

Sometimes in my life I look to people, retail therapy, food, or media consumption in an attempt to quench my spiritual longing, and it feels good in the moment. However, when I live on a diet of soul junk food, the spiritual flab begins to affect my health. While the consequences may not present themselves immediately, the plaque slowly builds in the arteries of my relationship with God. Apathy, bitterness, or distance in my relationship with God can slip in unnoticed until a crisis or conflict uncovers their presence.

Settling for counterfeits brings consequences that affect our spiritual health and keep us from the good plans God has for us. As we keep our focus on God—the "real deal"—we can then more easily spot the fakes in our lives. God wants to give us Himself in the midst of a world that offers every kind of substitute.

Resources

How we spend our money is a great indicator of what we value. When we put God first in our lives, we give generously to others rather than indulge our own wants and desires. Jeremiah gave this message from God to Jehoiakim, the king of Judah:

> *"But a beautiful cedar palace does not make a great king!*
>> *Your father, Josiah, also had plenty to eat and drink.*
> *But he was just and right in all his dealings.*
>> *That is why God blessed him.*
> *He gave justice and help to the poor and needy, and everything went well for him.*
> ***Isn't that what it means to know me?"***
>> *says the LORD.*
>>>> Jeremiah 22:15-16 (emphasis added)

When we know God and put Him first in our lives, we should want to help the poor and needy.

Approximately 21,000-plus children die every day across the globe of preventable diseases.[1] While that number fluctuates a little from year to year, I am astounded to realize that this number can be compared to one hundred commercial airplanes carrying two hundred children each crashing every day. We can't "fix it." Poverty is complex and widespread. So what does God want us to do? After reading Jeremiah's messages to the people, I know what God wants us not to do, and that's ignore it. Though our response might look different for each of us, God calls us to care for those in need.

Speaking through Jeremiah, God had this to say about the people of Judah:

> *"From the least to the greatest,*
> > *their lives are ruled by greed.*
> *From prophets to priests,*
> > *they are all frauds."*
>
> Jeremiah 6:13

We do not have to be like them—ruled by our greed. We can choose to lay aside our idols of consumption. And as we do, we will uncover resources that we can use to help others. As we examine our lives and spending habits, we'll find small sacrifices each of us can make to help those in need—in our own communities and around the world.

Making a Fake

Envision with me the women of Judah. They might have been drawing water from the well, preparing food in an outdoor kitchen shared by neighbors, or sitting around weaving cloth or sewing clothes. They reminisced about the stories of God from the past and surmised that their God must have lost His power because much bigger nations had become the playmakers with all the wealth, power, and control. So, logically, they determined that the gods of those nations must be stronger.

Instead of clinging to the God of their ancestors, the women of Judah decided to get themselves some new gods. Oh, they weren't original gods. These women decided their religion was outdated and needed a modern makeover. So what if they tweaked it a little to make it better by incorporating some foreign gods and religious practices? After all, we women are skilled at making suggestions on how to do things better. However, when it comes to the sovereign ruler of the universe, we must worship Him alone and dare to hope in His way over ours. When addressing the people's idolatry, Jeremiah said this:

> *"Their gods are like*
>> *helpless scarecrows in a cucumber field!*
> *They cannot speak,*
>> *and they need to be carried because they*
>> *cannot walk.*
> *Do not be afraid of such gods,*
>> *for they can neither harm you nor do you*
>> *any good."*

> LORD, *there is no one like you!*
> *For you are great, and your name is full of*
> *power.*
>
> Jeremiah 10:5-6

If we will take a good look in the spiritual mirror, we'll see that we are not that different from the women of Judah. We, too, sometimes create our own version of God that isn't consistent with what His Word reveals.

If we really believe God is who He says He is in His Word, then we will pray more and manipulate less. Sometimes our attitudes, actions, and lack of prayer reveal that we are making our own backups instead of trusting fully in God's ability to care for us. Often we fashion a god that doesn't intervene, a god that's involved only in the "big" things instead of the details, a god who is waiting for us to mess up. That is a counterfeit god—not the true and living God.

The best way to get rid of these idols in our lives is to offer them up to God. As we study His Word, talk to Him, and deepen our relationship, we will see our idols for the counterfeits they are in light of the greatness of our God.

3.

Opening Our Ears

Listening

It happened one night when I was with the gals at middle school youth group. They were sharing some communication issues they all seemed to be having with their parents. The resounding response went like this: "My parents don't listen. When I talk, I can see they are thinking about something else. They are busy, preoccupied, and my school or friend problems aren't important to them. Eventually, I just quit telling them all the details because they don't listen anyway or they act like the things I'm concerned about are silly or unimportant."

This composite of multiple responses alarmed me. When I went home and sat down with my daughters to inquire about my own listening skills, I found they had similar feelings. I began to wonder: if my listening skills are lacking with my own children who are physically present and asking for my attention, how much easier is it for me to struggle with listening to my Creator God?

How about you? Are your spiritual ears open or closed? In studying Jeremiah, I see a resounding theme that occurs over and over. God wants His people to open their ears and listen to Him:

"Ask me and I will tell you remarkable secrets you do not know about things to come."

Jeremiah 33:3

Let's explore this theme in Jeremiah and some of the ways we can become better listeners in our relationship with God.

Called to Listen

As we read through Jeremiah's book, we can't help but notice the volume of references to listening. Time and time again Jeremiah writes about God longing for His people to listen to Him. On one occasion, Jeremiah even addresses the women specifically:

Listen, you women, to the words of the LORD;
  open your ears to what he has to say.

Jeremiah 9:20a

The Hebrew word for listen is *shama*, and it means "to hear with attention or interest."[2] This isn't a casual kind of listening while looking at a phone or thinking through a grocery list. To have biblical "open ears" means to listen, respond, cooperate, maintain focus, and prove with your actions that you have heard what God is saying.

We, too, struggle with closed spiritual ears, don't we? Despite the gifts of God's living Word, His Spirit, His body of believers (the church), and the life of His beloved Son, we often find ourselves distracted and stubborn like the peers of Jeremiah. God is calling us to open our ears and be willing to hear.

Would those closest to you describe you as quick to listen, responsive, cooperative, focused, and living a life that reflects the faith you claim?

Reading with Curiosity

Another way we listen to God is by reading His Word with curiosity. Do you remember the Curious George children's books? The man with the yellow hat often got frustrated with Curious George, but George's curiosity helped save the day on many occasions. We can learn from this little monkey to approach God's Word with an inquisitive posture.

Rather than reading the Bible out of routine, obligation, or preparation for a lesson, what if we studied it with the intent of knowing God better? We could ask questions such as these:

- What will I learn about God—who He is, how He interacts with people, what the verses say about His character?
- What will I learn about myself—how I approach God, what He calls me to do/not do, how He expresses His love, what keeps me from experiencing Him more fully?
- Is there anything that God is specifically saying about my current thoughts, attitudes, or actions?

As we seek to know God through His Word, we'll find He is the Potter and we are the clay. We'll see Him as the Lord of Heaven's Armies. We'll also find that Jeremiah knew Him as the Sovereign Lord for whom nothing is too difficult:

"O Sovereign LORD! You made the heavens and earth by your strong hand and powerful arm. Nothing is too hard for you!"

Jeremiah 32:17

We can listen and know God better, too, as we study His Word curiously.

Cling Like Underwear

Another way we become better listeners is by clinging to God.

Do you like loose, baggy underwear? I don't either. Underwear doesn't look or feel good unless it fits snugly. Guys may choose between boxers and briefs, but we girls like our underwear to fit.

You might be wondering where this talk of underwear is going. Believe me, this Texas girl does not enjoy public conversations of private things. It doesn't take much to make me blush. However, God is the One who mentions the "unmentionables." He tells Jeremiah to go bury a new loincloth (underwear) in a hole. He then uses it as an illustration for how He created His people to be close to Him—to cling to Him.

> *"As a loincloth clings to a man's waist, so I created Judah and Israel to cling to me, says the LORD. They were to be my people, my pride, my glory—an honor to my name. But they would not listen to me."*

Jeremiah 13:11

Unfortunately, the people of Judah refused to listen. I pray our response will be different. I hope we will be tight, personal, and daily in our relationship with our God—clinging like underwear.

Listen to the Right Voices

Besides reading God's Word with curiosity and clinging closely to Him in a daily relationship, becoming a better listener requires that we listen to the right voices. Every day we are bombarded by different voices. Between my mailbox, social media feeds, television shows, and daily interactions with others—even as I wait in the checkout line at the store—there is a constant barrage of information coming at me. There's no shortage of voices in the Christian realm either. It's great to talk, debate, and work through the issues related to trying to follow God. But how can we know that we are following the right leaders, listening to the right voices, and walking in God's truth in the many arenas of life? We don't want to be like the people of Judah in Jeremiah's day who didn't listen to God but, instead, chose to listen to "others" with a more popular message.

Jeremiah teaches us some principles of discernment:

- Consider the moral character of the messenger.

- Evaluate the message to see if it lines up with God's Word.
- Ask the right questions.

He said that not every message nourishes our soul with truth. Some information is helpful, like grain, and other information is more like straw—it might provide a temporary comfort for laying your head but will still leave you with an empty spiritual stomach.

> *"Let these false prophets tell their dreams,*
> *but let my true messengers faithfully*
> *proclaim my every word.*
> *There is a difference between straw and*
> *grain!"*
>
> Jeremiah 23:28

As we listen to God, we need God's wisdom to know the difference between straw and grain. He will help us discern what will nourish our soul with truth and what will give us momentary comfort, but leave us empty.

Keep Asking

Jeremiah modeled listening for us. We see that he approached God with confidence, rehearsing characteristics about who God is and how He behaves. He asked specific questions. He expressed his frustrations over things that didn't make sense to him. He admitted his own faults and asked God to correct him when he was wrong.

God welcomes our asking too. Asking means dialogue. We don't have to stuff our doubts. Doubts are real, and everyone has them. What is most important is what we do with them. When we doubt, it should lead us to think, study, and ask questions.

I write specific questions I have for God all the time. I write them in my Bible next to a passage I don't understand. I write them in my journal as I pray. I once asked God why the Book of Jeremiah seems like it isn't in order since it doesn't flow chronologically. Not five minutes later in my daily reading I found Ecclesiastes 7:13: "Accept the way God does things, / for who can straighten what he has made crooked?" Yep. Got it God—I don't need to straighten You out!

If God doesn't answer right away, keep asking. Then take time to listen with the expectation that He will answer. Jeremiah wrote about the value of waiting on God:

Can any of the worthless foreign gods send us rain?

> *Does it fall from the sky by itself?*

No, you are the one, O LORD our God!
    Only you can do such things.
    So we will wait for you to help us.

                      Jeremiah 14:22

We see the consistency of asking, listening, and knowing God in prayer all the way from Jeremiah through the entire span of the New Testament. This is a consistent theme. Ask, ask, and ask. Listen, listen, and listen some more!

God mostly answers my questions through His Word, but He sometimes uses other books, people, and circumstances. When God seems silent in my life, I usually find it is because I've either stopped asking questions or stopped taking the time to listen for the answers.

What is keeping you from a close relationship with God in your prayer life? What is He saying to you today?

4.

Staying Spiritually Sensitive

Heart Issues

Have you ever experienced spiritual chest pain? You ache inside over emotions you can't readily identify. All you know is that something hurts. Physically, hearts can experience any number of problems, such as leaky valves, aneurysms, or clogged arteries. Similarly, we have fragile hearts spiritually.

No matter what our heart issues are right now, we must be careful to allow God full access to our hearts. Glossing over issues, skipping to the next thing, and moving on in life without dealing with heart issues is much simpler than going through the softening process. Many of us have done this for years—especially in relationships with family and friends. We stuff our pain and continue living our lives without dealing with our heart issues. The great news is that allowing God to do the deep work fosters closeness with Him in the midst of our brokenness that is unbelievably worth it.

Jeremiah was no stranger to spiritual open heart surgery. He endured rejection, betrayal, and taunting by his own people when he chose to follow God wholeheartedly. Yet he remained humble and teachable in the midst of his struggles. How did he do it? What can we learn from his message and example?

Heart Evaluation

For starters, we have to embrace the truth about our human heart defaults and give ourselves a regular heart evaluation. Listen to what God said about the heart to the prophet Jeremiah:

"The human heart is the most deceitful of all things,
> *and desperately wicked.*
> *Who really knows how bad it is?*
But I, the Lord, search all hearts
> *and examine secret motives.*

I give all people their due rewards,
according to what their actions deserve."
Jeremiah 17:9-10

I can be an expert heart evaluator—of other
people's motives and heart attitudes, that is. If I
don't check myself regularly, I find that I read into
every word, expression, and body language cue to
form a conclusion about how the other person feels
and thinks; and I may be off course. With relationships, finances, and disagreements, we can all be
too quick to see where others are wrong.

Through Jeremiah's prophecy we see that God
says He is the One who searches all hearts and
examines secret motives. Focusing on others' heart
issues wastes time and distracts us from dealing
with our own heart symptoms. But when we spend
our mental and emotional energy allowing God to
evaluate the sin in our hearts first, we usually find
that we see others and their situations differently.
By being aware of our personal tendencies toward
sin and expending our time and energy on our own
repentance, we can view others with more grace
and less judgment. The prayer of the psalmist
should become our regular personal prayer:

Search me, O God, and know my heart;
test me and know my anxious thoughts.

Point out anything in me that offends you,
*   and lead me along the path of everlasting life.*
                                    Psalm 139:23-24

Behavior Modification vs. Heart Change

After taking some time to evaluate our hearts, our tendency is to go into "change my behavior mode." We say to ourselves, "Okay, now that I see the hardness, bitterness, and deception in my heart, I will get up every day and have my quiet time, go to church every Sunday (even when I'm tired), and try to watch less TV. That should help change my heart." However, when we over concentrate on actions, we don't get to the root heart issues.

We must be careful not to try to fix ourselves by trying to follow rules in an attempt to clean up our hearts. That is not what God has in mind. Heart change happens internally first and then displays itself externally as we acknowledge and respond to the sin we've identified.

God instructed His people about heart change through the prophet Jeremiah:

Therefore, go and give this message to Israel. This is what the LORD says:
*   "O Israel, my faithless people,*
*   come home to me again,*

> *for I am merciful.*
> > *I will not be angry with you forever.*
> *Only acknowledge your guilt.*
> > *Admit that you rebelled against the*
> > LORD *your God*
> *and committed adultery against him*
> > *by worshiping idols under every*
> > *green tree.*
> *Confess that you refused to listen to my voice.*
> *I, the* LORD, *have spoken!"*
>
> Jeremiah 3:12-13

In these verses, Jeremiah presents three truths that lead to lasting change in life:

- Know it. Get honest with ourselves about how we feel and the sin tendencies we have.
- Share it. Bring it before a loving God who longs to offer us hope and healing.
- Own it. Accept personal responsibility for our mistakes—and accept the forgiveness God offers.

We can know, share, and own our sin because God in His mercy will forgive us and help us turn from it. He doesn't ask us to clean ourselves up, fix our bad behavior, and then approach Him. He welcomes us in our brokenness. He alone can change our hearts.

Where Do Broken Hearts Go?

Finding out I was having twins just ten days before I had them caused great fear in this gal who'd already experienced the birth of a singleton. I knew what to expect. The thought of doubling that encounter freaked me right out!

Sometimes our trials are not physical experiences, such as birthing a child, but are emotional, mental, and spiritual labors. Such trials are able to birth great intimacy with Christ, but the process can be excruciating. Jeremiah knew this all too well as he is often referred to as the Weeping Prophet—rejected by his family and community, falsely accused and imprisoned, thrown into the bottom of a muddy pit, and found weeping over his people who refused to repent.

When we experience deep pain, we are vulnerable to bitterness, depression, and anxiety. God calls us to bring our broken hearts to Him:

> *"My wayward children," says the* Lord,
> > *"come back to me, and I will heal your*
> > *wayward hearts."*

> *"Yes, we're coming," the people reply,*
> > *"for you are the* Lord *our God."*
>
> Jeremiah 3:22

Throughout his book, Jeremiah leads by example in showing us how to bring our hurting hearts to the Great Physician who soothes and heals as He mends our broken places.

Guard Your Heart

Because our hearts are so sensitive, we must be careful to guard them. The Bible tells us,

> *Guard your heart above all else,*
> *for it determines the course of your life.*
> Proverbs 4:23

In a world that offers easy and instant access to an overwhelming amount of information, guarding our hearts takes great intentionality. With remotes, keyboards, and touch screens increasing our exposure to harmful influences, we can easily become desensitized. God longs for us to keep our hearts soft so that we are grieved when inappropriate behaviors are considered acceptable. He asks us to guard what we allow to flow both in and out of our hearts. Allowing the Holy Spirit and God's Word to be our "filter" helps keep our words and actions from damaging our hearts. Jeremiah said his people had lost their ability to blush. They became desensitized by the surrounding culture and failed to protect their hearts. He cautioned the people about how their thoughts and words might influence their hearts.

When was the last time you really considered your heart boundaries? How can obedience to God's standards provide protection for your heart?

With All Your Heart

Finally, we must remember that God doesn't want half of our hearts. We have to be careful not to resemble the people of Judah in Jeremiah's day. They gave God their leftovers. When the people lost faith in God's power, and perhaps even His very existence, they kept the best for themselves and put their rotten leftovers in the offering baskets at the Temple.

Similarly, our offerings to God reveal what we really believe about Him. We often put more time and intentionality into planning our next vacation or birthday party than we do intensely pursuing God with our whole hearts. While offering God our leftovers, we wonder why we often seem to be losing the spiritual battle against sin in our lives.

Jeremiah wrote that God desires us to pursue Him wholeheartedly.

"If you look for me wholeheartedly, you will find me."

Jeremiah 29:13

When we do, we will find the relationship we were created to enjoy—even in our pain.

Dealing with heart issues isn't always easy. Many of us have been hurt deeply by others, whether through abuse, neglect, or rejection. Others of us may not have suffered as much, but we still need to work through the daily wear and tear on our hearts as we live in a fallen world. God offers us hope and healing as we surrender our broken hearts to Him. God calls us to trust Him and dare to hope in Him—even with the most fragile of hearts. He promises that when we seek Him, we will find Him. And His hope never leads to disappointment!

5.

Quitting the Blame Game

Personal Responsibility

Who's your favorite "target"? When things go wrong in my world, I can find lots of places to assign blame. My husband, the church, or anyone standing next to me at the moment might find my finger pointed at them as responsible for my failure.

We come by this tendency quite honestly. Adam blamed Eve, and Eve accused the serpent at the scene of the very first sin. Ever since then, we have had to fight the urge to blame and have had to learn to take personal responsibility for our mistakes. God doesn't want us to grovel in shame but simply admit our shortcomings so that we can be forgiven and changed through His power.

The people of Judah wouldn't listen to Jeremiah's call to take personal responsibility. They continued to play the blame game. God called them to let go of their prideful attitude:

This is what the LORD says:
"Don't let the wise boast in their wisdom,
 or the powerful boast in their power,
 or the rich boast in their riches.
But those who wish to boast
 should boast in this alone:
that they truly know me and understand that I am
the LORD. . . ."

Jeremiah 9:23-24

As we look to Jeremiah's book, let's see if we can learn from their mistakes and take a posture of humility instead of pride.

Good Discipline

Nothing can get under a parent's skin like a child who won't respond to appropriate discipline. One of my children says that another is to blame for his or her failure to complete a chore or make a wise choice. Then when I investigate and point out the blaming child's own sin or failure in the situation, the blame can quickly turn to me. I'm told that I make unfair decisions, expect too much, or don't understand their preteen lives. My discipline or consequences are viewed as measures to "ruin their lives." Over and over I try to explain that if I didn't care, I wouldn't take the time and energy to correct, train, pray, and discipline.

While I try to parent as best as possible, I don't always get it right. However, God is the perfect parent. His kids often rebelled, but He continued to give them clear warnings and to follow through with consequences when they didn't respond.

> *"Is not Israel still my son,*
>   *my darling child?" says the* LORD.
> *"I often have to punish him,*
>   *but I still love him.*
> *That's why I long for him*
>   *and surely will have mercy on him."*
>
> Jeremiah 31:20

God does the same with us. He isn't out to ruin our lives, but He does ask us to trust that He is working out the right combination of mercy and justice on His perfect timetable.

Finding a Target

When I was a kid, my dad occasionally would wake everyone in the house and call us to hunt for

47

his lost keys so that he could leave for work. The apple doesn't fall far from the tree—only with me it's my cell phone. I never remember where I left it and often blame my kids or husband for moving it. Usually I find it in my purse or jacket pocket—right where I left it. Until it is found, I am sure that someone else is to blame. It's humbling when the facts prove that my accusations are unfounded.

The people of Judah had problems with blaming as well. They often claimed they were innocent of wrongdoing and denied that they worshiped idols. They did not want to take personal responsibility for playing a part in the consequences headed their way. Jeremiah gave them this warning:

> *"People from many nations will pass by the ruins of this city and say to one another, 'Why did the Lord destroy such a great city?' And the answer will be, 'Because they violated their covenant with the Lord their God by worshiping other gods.'"*
>
> Jeremiah 22:8-9

What are your targets for blame shifting when things go wrong in your world? What freedom could you find in admitting your faults instead of playing the blame game?

Perilous Pride

Admitting our faults requires letting go of pride. Pride is an elusive thing. It can take many forms. Simply put, it is an obsession with self. Apart from God's work in our lives, every one of us will make decisions to serve our own interests—to paint ourselves in the best light and work out situations to our benefit. This is the core of our sin problem. We all battle daily against the sin of pride.

Jeremiah pronounced judgments on the surrounding nations of Judah, and many of them were indicted for their pride. He wrote,

> *And if you still refuse to listen,*
> > *I will weep alone because of your pride.*
> *My eyes will overflow with tears,*
> > *because the LORD's flock will be led away*
> > *into exile.*

> Jeremiah 13:17

God wept over the people of Judah's downfall of trusting in their "wealth and skill." They deceived themselves into thinking that every good thing in their lives was their own doing. This attitude resembles the American mind-sets of "I deserve it," "I am powerful," and "Look at all I have accomplished." Hard work, goal setting, and material goods are not inherently wrong, but we would be wise to remember that anything good we accomplish originated in God, who gave us the talent and resources.

Who do you credit for the successes in your life? In what ways do you find pride creeping into your thoughts, attitudes, and actions?

Going Through the Motions

Pride also can affect our devotion to God. Though religious rituals can have great significance and can be holy acts through which we experience the presence and grace of God, we must be careful not to allow them to make us feel that we are somehow "appeasing" God or fulfilling some kind of duty or obligation. Religious rituals become empty when our motivation is anything other than our devoted love for God.

That's exactly what had happened to the people of Judah's worship: they were going through the motions. The priests were offering sacrifices, and false prophets were delivering messages they said were from the Lord; but their hearts were not right. Jeremiah delivered this warning:

"Don't be fooled into thinking that you will never suffer because the Temple is here. It's a lie!

Do you really think you can steal, murder, commit adultery, lie, and burn incense to Baal and all those other new gods of yours, and then come here and stand before me in my Temple and chant, 'We are safe!'—only to go right back to all those evils again?"

Jeremiah 7:8-10

Can you think of seasons in your spiritual life when you have been going through the motions? I have found myself reading the Bible, serving in ministry, or even attending church out of duty. While some spiritual disciplines require pushing through emotions of resistance, we must be careful not to allow our walk with God to become routine and empty.

What can you do to breathe new life into your methods of connecting with God?

Rescue with Repentance

The good news for us is that it is never too late to change our ways.

Have you ever been driving the wrong way and your smart phone or GPS said, "Recalculating"? Then it rerouted you so that you were turned back toward your destination rather than away from it. A similar concept happens in life when we get off course spiritually. Once we acknowledge we are moving in the wrong direction, we must turn around—repent—and go God's new way, which gets us to the destination of intimacy with Him.

The people of Judah had a lot of experience in offering empty words. They cried out to God on several occasions, declaring their intent to change their ways, but there were no actions to back up their words. Jeremiah spoke often about repentance as a reorientation of one's life, that is, a turning away from sin and a simultaneous turning to God.

If closeness with God is your destination, are you on the most direct route to getting there? Is there any "recalculating" that you need to do to turn from sin and turn toward God?

We all need rescuing, don't we? We may not have the Babylonian army invading us, but I haven't met many women with problem-free lives. We all cry out from time to time asking for help with difficult relationships, relationship or marriage struggles, parenting challenges, draining people, financial crises, work issues, and endless daily tasks. It's no wonder we are looking for some reprieve. God longs for us to cry out to Him for help. Instead of blaming others, ourselves, or Him, God calls us to turn from our sin and walk in obedience.

> *This is what the LORD says:*
> *"Stop at the crossroads and look around.*
>> *Ask for the old, godly way, and walk in it.*
> *Travel its path, and you will find rest for your souls.*
>> *But you reply, 'No, that's not the road we want!'"*
>
> Jeremiah 6:16

God is always faithful to redirect us as we take personal responsibility for our mistakes and ask for His help in navigating our path in life.

6.

Finding the Source of Our Hope

The Promised Messiah

We cannot escape this haunting feeling as we turn the pages of Jeremiah: the days of his prophecy sound uncannily similar to ours. While the symptoms may flesh out differently, the root problems of our modern culture profoundly parallel those of the nation of Judah. Like the Judeans, we face a choice as individuals and as a nation to respond to God's call to hope. While despair seems to loom all around us, we can find hope. While our circumstances, conflicts, and problems may not improve, our hope is found in God's promised Messiah. Jeremiah said that He would come and save the people from their sin under a new covenant.

While some days we may have to be very daring to continue to hope, we can join Jeremiah in trusting that God will come through for us:

"For I know the plans I have for you," says the LORD. "They are plans for good and not for disaster, to give you a future and a hope."

Jeremiah 29:11

Let's see what good future God has in store for us and how the promised Messiah—known to us as Jesus—is the best part of God's plan for us.

An Audience of One

Whether it is little insecurities about what others think about an outfit or big decisions that tempt us to trust in things we can see and control rather than in God, fearing people and circumstances will always get us into big trouble. Living to please the spectators on the road of faith leads to manipulation, worry, and disappointment—and ultimately to discipline from a loving God who wants to lead us back to Him as our source of hope.

We need to evaluate what is bigger in our lives: people and circumstances, or God? When we live like Jeremiah, putting fear of God over fear of people or circumstances, the road is not problem-free but it is blessed. When we live to please others, we might please some people but disappoint others in the process.

When those stones of disapproval come flying at you, as they inevitably will, remember there is one Spectator who is crazy about you. His name is Jesus, and He wants you to follow His path because He adores you and knows the dangers of the approval roller coaster. What decisions are you facing today? Who are you looking to please in your choices? I pray you'll look to an audience of One who longs to bless you as you dare to live His way. Always remember,

Fear of the L ORD is the foundation of true knowledge,
> *but fools despise wisdom and discipline.*
Proverbs 1:7

While people may let us down, God's promises never fail. He promised to send us a Savior because sin separates us from Him. Jeremiah taught about this promised Messiah that would bring us hope.

Good Plans Ahead

No matter how bleak things may seem, God can work even the worst of circumstances together for our good. Jeremiah 29:11 says that God has good plans ahead for His people. However, in the verse right before it, we find that His people will be in exile for seventy years:

This is what the LORD says: "You will be in Babylon for seventy years. But then I will come and do for you all the good things I have promised, and I will bring you home again."

Jeremiah 29:10

Jeremiah 29:11 is not a promise to make life problem-free. It is an assurance to love and bless us even when times are tough.

God wants to bless us—to give us rest, hope, and peace. And these are good plans! However, because God knows that we cannot have these things apart from Him and that we are prone to wander, sometimes He allows difficult circumstances so that we will come back to Him. God knows and understands our bent toward sin. That's why He sent Jesus as a sacrifice, prophesying about Him through Jeremiah so many years before His coming. Ultimately, God's best plan for all who follow Him is spending eternity with Him. Though in this life there is much suffering, in the next there will be no tears. Even if the world crumbles around us or we must face many years in a difficult circumstance, we can know with confidence that God's plans are good because one day we will see Him face to face. Talk about a future and a hope!

How can you see God bringing good out of a difficult situation in your life right now?

Hope That Brings Us Back

Even in the midst of the promised punishment for sin, we see God's longing for His people:

*Long ago the L*ORD *said to Israel:*
"I have loved you, my people, with an everlasting love.

> *With unfailing love I have drawn you to myself."*

Jeremiah 31:3

You see, God offers hope for a remnant who are willing to follow Him. This remnant is not a leftover piece of fabric. A remnant is a small group of people left over after some kind of disaster. Jeremiah also predicts a future day when God will bring a remnant of His people back to their Promised Land.

God often speaks of the remnant of His people with words of hope and compassion. They have been through a lot of difficulty, which has left them humble and ready to obey. These are the people who have learned to trust in Him through their struggles.

Even Jeremiah grew weary of suffering at times and got very discouraged. God continually encouraged him and called him to persevere in faith even when he didn't understand why no one seemed to be responding to his messages:

This is how the LORD responds:

> *"If you return to me, I will restore you*
>   *so you can continue to serve me.*
> *If you speak good words rather than worthless ones,*
>   *you will be my spokesman.*
> *You must influence them;*
>   *do not let them influence you!"*
>   Jeremiah 15:19

Take heart: you are in good company! No matter if your world seems unstable in every direction, God offers you hope even through your pain. Like Jeremiah, some of our greatest times of intimacy with God come in moments of desperation when we realize how dependent on Him we truly are.

Where have you found God's nearness in your struggles? Even if you are far from Him today, He is calling you with hope to bring you back to Him.

The Promised Messiah

We find the hope of the promised Messiah throughout Jeremiah's writings. Jeremiah didn't

know His name but referred to Him as the Lord
Is Our Righteousness, Who would save the people
from sin.

> *"For the time is coming,"*
>   *says the LORD,*
> *"when I will raise up a righteous descendant*
>   *from King David's line.*
> *He will be a King who rules with wisdom.*
>   *He will do what is just and right through-*
>   *out the land.*
> *And this will be his name:*
>   *'The LORD Is Our Righteousness.'*
> *In that day Judah will be saved,*
>   *and Israel will live in safety."*

Jeremiah 23:5-6

God gave Jeremiah glimpses of a new covenant
of grace and hope through this promised Messiah.
While Jeremiah didn't know every detail about the
cross, the crown of thorns, or the Resurrection, he
still placed his hope in this future Messiah. The
sacrifices, the Temple, the priesthood, and many
of the other religious practices all pointed to Jesus.

We have the privilege of reading Jeremiah's
prophecies from this side of the cross. We see the
fulfillment of his words. We find the source of our
hope in Christ, the One who paid the price for your

sin and mine. Our hope is built on Him alone. His death and resurrection give us a reason to hope in this life and the next. When we choose to fix our minds on Jesus, it gives us perspective for everything else we are going through.

How can you apply the gospel to your situation and find hope even in the midst of your suffering?

Full Access

What does knowing Jesus mean to you?

Think about this: if you could have access to a great Christian leader in our day, who would it be? Now imagine if that person gave you his or her personal phone number and said, "Call or text me anytime you have questions or are struggling. I will pray for you, counsel you, and encourage you." Would you lose the number and never contact the person, or would you call often to build a relationship?

The question facing us is this: are we taking full advantage of our full access to the One who is our source of hope? Others can help us, but that doesn't even compare to what God offers us through a relationship with Him. Although sin separates us from God, Christ restores our relationship through His sacrifice on the cross. So now we can enjoy friendship with a holy God. How can you take more advantage of the full access you've been given through Christ?

Jeremiah poured out his heart to God. He asked questions, listened for answers, softened his heart, and dared to hope even when life circumstances seemed to go from bad to worse. In the Book of Lamentations, which Jeremiah also wrote, he made this bold declaration:

> *Yet I still dare to hope*
>   *when I remember this:*
>
> *The faithful love of the LORD never ends!*
>   *His mercies never cease.*
> *Great is his faithfulness;*
>   *his mercies begin afresh each morning.*
>   Lamentations 3:21-23

Jeremiah dared to hope even in an unstable world. His messages about surrender, idolatry, listening, heart issues, personal responsibility, and hope in the promised Messiah hit very close to home as we attempt to navigate the difficulties in our own lives. Even if your circumstances do not budge an inch or perhaps intensify, I pray that your hope grows because of God's steadfast love and new mercies.

Jeremiah dared to hope even when he found that all that he'd hoped for from the Lord was lost. Although some days can feel like we are in the bottom of a pit with Jeremiah, I have found that my greatest struggles have become some of God's greatest triumphs in my life. He has used these trials to draw me nearer to Him. I pray that this is true for you as well and that we can continue to dare to hope together through whatever tomorrow may bring.

Notes

1. "Today, around 21,000 children died around the world," Anup Shah, Global Issues, last modified September 24, 2011, http://www.globalissues.org/article/715/today-21000-children-died-around-the-world.
2. "Shama," http://www.biblestudytools.com/lexicons/hebrew/kjv/shama.html.

If you liked this book, you'll love the Bible study.

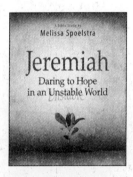

For more information about the study and Jeremiah Leader Kit (ISBN 978-1-4267-8897-0), visit **AbingdonWomen.com** or your favorite Christian retailer.